To remember
the "1981"
trip
and the
happiness
we share.

with love
and
thought—
Diane

Jan. 1981

CHARLESTON
Houses and Gardens

A row of stately mansions faces White Point Garden and
South Battery. The garden was laid out in 1838, but the land
has been known as "White Point" from early days when the
ground was white with oyster shells.

CHARLESTON

Houses & Gardens

TEXT BY
Evangeline Davis

PHOTOGRAPHS BY
N. Jane Iseley

Published by the PRESERVATION SOCIETY OF CHARLESTON
Charleston, South Carolina

*Dedicated to the memory of
Miss Susan Pringle Frost*

Foreword

FORMATION of The Preservation Society of Charleston in 1920 has resulted in the preservation of many of the city's early, historic landmarks.

The Society's Constitution states its purpose as ". . . to cultivate and encourage interest in the preservation of buildings, sites and structures of historical significance or aesthetic significance, and to take whatever steps may be necessary and feasible to prevent the destruction or defacement of any such building, site or structure, such purpose being solely eleemosynary and not for profit."

In its earliest years, largely through the influence and work of Miss Susan Pringle Frost, the Society was responsible for the rehabilitation of Rainbow Row and several renovations on the east end of Tradd Street, Bedons Alley and Elliott Street.

These kinds of projects have continued, made possible by contributions and membership dues. Currently, there are over 1500 members. It is hoped that as the recognition of the inestimable value of preservation grows, the Society's membership also will expand.

The Preservation Society is indebted to, and wishes to express its thanks to, the many residents who opened their houses and gardens to the writer and photographer of this book.

Proceeds from the sale of this book will be used solely for furthering the work of the Society.

THE PRESERVATION SOCIETY OF CHARLESTON
Box 521   Charleston, S.C. 29402

Dawn breaking over Charleston harbor, as seen from St. Michael's steeple. The spectacular view is seaward toward the southeast, past Fort Sumter near the harbor entrance.

FOR THREE HUNDRED YEARS, as cultural capital of the American South, Charleston has treasured its traditions—in architecture and gardens, in cuisine, speech, leisure and intellectual pursuits, the simple joys of daily life.

Two noted twentieth century journalists agreed emphatically on the city's spirit. "Charleston," said William Allen White, "is the most civilized town in the world." Jonathan Daniels said he knew of no people with "a clearer sense of the tempo of good manners and good living."

Almost alone among the nation's cities Charleston has resisted the intrusion of glass-steel-concrete towers in its mid-city blocks. Instead, the heart of the old city has been renewed by faithful restorations, and energetic local leadership has preserved the appearance of early Charleston to a remarkable degree. Fanny Kemble, who noted an "air of decay" in 1836 and said it was a "genteel infirmity, as might be that of a distressed elderly gentlewoman," would be amazed that the lady has such renewed life. In any case, today's city is a wonderland for visitors seeking a glimpse of the American past.

The city was founded in 1670. Despite devastating fires, hurricanes, tornadoes, earthquakes, bombardment by guns from land and sea, a limited march of "progress" that ripped down some landmarks, and two enemy occupations, a surprising number of early buildings survive:

Seventy-three are pre-Revolutionary.

One hundred and thirty-six are late eighteenth century and post-Revolutionary.

Six hundred and twenty-three others were built before 1840.

At least twenty-six of these are considered of national importance.

The variety of these buildings is notable—from the simple charm of the Pink House to the imposing row of mansions fronting the Battery; from stark

One of the original fire insurance markers.

An earthquake bolt secures one end of a rod run through a building to give protection. These were installed after the severe quake of 1886.

and simple lines of single houses to columned Greek Revival facades; from the stuccoed brick walls of the old Powder Magazine to the elegance of St. Michael's Church.

There is the Miles Brewton House, one of the truly fine Georgian homes in the nation. There is also "Catfish Row", the prototype of a setting for DuBose Heyward's *Porgy* which joined American folklore as the Heyward-Gershwin musical *Porgy and Bess*. There are the Pirates' Houses, of Bermuda stone, where legend has it that buccaneers lived; and there is the Heyward-Washington House, where the first President was once a guest. Rainbow Row, once the homes and shops of prosperous merchants degenerated into slums, but the Daniel Ravenel House has been occupied by descendants of the eighteenth century owner all through the years.

There is a perpetual play of contrasting scale—between steeples and gambrel roofs, between thin-shanked 'single houses' turned sidewise to the street and waterfront mansions, between narrow, crooked alleys and the broad sweep of the harbor, between intimate walled gardens and the larger White Point Garden beneath its grove of live oaks.

But perhaps the secret of Charleston's architectural charm is in the loving, uncompromising attention to detail that has marked the building of the city from the start. It is not by accident that the urbane taste of early Charlestonians is reflected in today's city—and that these reflections are seldom pretentious despite an obvious, distinctive style evident on every hand.

An early drawing of the city shows literally hundreds of balconies, many of them of fine wrought iron. Those that escaped fires and wars and survived later collectors who descended upon the city attest to the early devotion to decorative detail. Other small but important triumphs of design and the builders' arts may be seen in cornices and gable ends, chimney pots and roof tiles, cobblestone pavings and curved stone steps, boot scrapers and stair rails, brass locks and arched fanlights. The almost dazzling array of columns and their capitals—chaste, ornate or rococo—the finish of the masonry forming houses, walls and gateposts, the exquisite use of scale and proportion, are all testimonials to the skills of builders and artisans.

Charleston was one of British America's first planned cities. The "Grand Modell" for the settlement called Charles Town was laid out with 375 lots and two Great Streets around 1673—and certainly before 1680—on a marshy tongue of land between two rivers. The plan had defects but the city was tastefully developed and was the early beneficiary of the straightforward, unassuming attitudes of its creators.

Nathaniel Heyward once refused to contribute toward a new local industry for fear it would "ruin the town for what it was intended to be, a summer home for rice planters." Heyward was a wealthy rice planter, himself, and his town house was a haven from the rigors of summer in the Low Country.

The first settlers arrived in 1670 in three small ships sent by the Lords Proprietors, loyal supporters of Charles II. These men were the first rulers of their vast domains in the Carolina wilderness. On the advice of an Indian Chief, some 147 Englishmen settled on the western bank of the Ashley River; but the "Towne of Trade" was soon moved to the large peninsula lying between the Ashley and Cooper Rivers. With passing years, it became obvious that the founders had chosen a strategic spot from which the southeastern United States was to be developed.

Within twelve years of the first landing, the town boasted more than a hundred houses, and before the end of the second decade the first church had been built—the original St. Philip's. Charleston grew rapidly into the dominant port of the Eastern Seaboard and commerce began to enrich its merchants and entrepreneurs—first through Indian trade based on skins, and later in timber and naval stores, indigo, rice and finally cotton.

Large original holdings were purchased both in the Low Country and in the endless forest lands surrounding the tidewater; in the beginning, land sold for a penny an acre and far-sighted men of means quickly took advantage of the bargain.

By 1700, the area produced "more rice than we had ships to transport", and thirty years later the fantastically rich plantations produced 40,000 barrels of golden-hued rice yearly. It was 1830 before the great tide of prosperity reached its peak however, with the advent of the cotton gin and an efficient new method of irrigating the rice fields.

The city survived threats from the Spanish colonies to the south, Indian wars, siege and occupation during the Revolution, and long bombardment during what is generally known as the

Ingenuity in building that saves brick also forms an unusually beautiful wall of Charleston design.

141 and 143-145 Church Street. These two houses were, according to legend, used by pirates in the days when they were tolerated, if not welcome, in the city. They are built of "Bermuda stone", coral limestone blocks cut in Bermuda. Both houses are pre-Revolutionary.

Civil War but is still referred to in Charleston as the War Between the States.

It also survived natural disasters: tornadoes and hurricanes of frightening intensity (during one, a ship with a nine-foot draft was thrown far into the town), earthquakes, yellow fever, malaria. Fires laid waste many acres in 1740, 1778, 1796, 1838 and 1861.

Religious tolerance that was to influence the future attracted many settlers; among them were Huguenot refugees who were to add immeasurably to the tempo and quality of life. The Huguenots had begun a "French Church" by 1681. There were Quakers during the early years. Jews were granted citizenship by an Act of the Colonial Assembly in 1697. Congregationalists, Presbyterians and Baptists were also welcomed.

The city's early homes, though showing English origins and traditions, were so ingeniously adapted to the sub-tropical climate of the Carolina coast as to influence local building across the centuries.

One result was the "single house", a house one room wide, two rooms on each floor, one end turned to the street, and sited to catch the prevailing breeze. Native historian Samual Gaillard Stoney has depicted the typical Charleston house as simply a hot weather dwelling that is also habitable in winter. The houses of the city, he says, lie like a sailing fleet, trimmed to "the sacred Charleston wind that every hot afternoon blows up from the southwest across the Ashley River and cools off the town for the evening." This weather pattern was the reason long piazzas were placed on the south and west fronts of the single houses—cool on summer evenings and warm on sunny winter mornings.

There are also "double houses", square ones usually (but with notable exceptions) with four rooms to a floor, some of them from the Georgian period, many influenced by the Adam style. As Mr. Stoney has said, the double house has its own peculiarities. "To get room for really sumptuous parlors it puts them upstairs where they can run over the space occupied below by a central hall, and where also their coved ceilings can be carried up into the roof space. As a rule the Double House is in every way more pretentious in its decorations than the Single House . . ."

The earliest of the city's houses, reflecting the simple tastes—and more limited incomes—of the first generations gave way to more sophisticated

90-92-94 Church Street. (Right to left) Fine examples of the Charleston "single house". The sidewalk door is in reality a formal entrance to the piazza; the actual front door is secluded from the street. These three houses date from 1730 to 1805.
Governor Joseph Alston and his wife, Theodosia Burr, lived at No. 94.

ones after 1720, the year the British Crown assumed control of the colony. By 1750, Charleston was known as "the richest and most eminent city in the southern part of North America . . . 1500 houses, regular streets and many fine buildings."

In an era of prosperity unbroken until the Revolution, Charlestonians built in the grand manner—St. Michael's Church, and mansions like those of Miles Brewton and Colonel John Stuart. After the Revolution, in an even greater tide of prosperity that followed a depression, the city's builders embraced the Adam style. From this period date the remarkable spiral stairs and oval, as well as octagonal, rooms, delicately decorated mantels and cornices.

Charleston's most celebrated architects worked after the Revolution. One of the most talented and best known was an "amateur" of independent means who produced designs for his family and friends. Gabriel Manigault was a descendant of an early Huguenot refugee; his earliest known house design is the Joseph Manigault House, which was built for his brother. His other work includes the South Carolina Society Hall and the City Hall.

Robert Mills, another native Charlestonian, was the first of the trained, professional architects known to have worked in the city. To him are attributed

100 Meeting Street. Fireproof Building. Completed in 1828, this structure was the work of architect Robert Mills, who used brick, stone and iron in what was the first attempt in this country to erect a completely fireproof building. It once was the County Records Building. Recently restored, it is occupied by the South Carolina Historical Society.

Intricate details of window cornices form interesting shadow patterns and also break direct sun rays on these Broad Street offices.

the Fireproof Building, the Marine Hospital and the First Baptist Church. (Mills was well known nationally and was the architect for the Washington Monument in the District of Columbia as well as buildings in Philadelphia, Baltimore, Richmond, Columbia, Mobile and New Orleans.)

E. B. White possibly was Charleston's most prolific architect. A number of his best buildings date to the 1840's. He designed, among others, the present Huguenot Church, Grace Church, Market Hall, the portico and wings of the College of Charleston and the St. Philip's Church steeple.

And to collaborate with architects and builders were iron workers in remarkable number, cabinetmakers who produced "Charleston pieces" by the score, wood carvers and highly skilled plasterers who fashioned the medallions and cornices to decorate the grand drawing rooms.

Along with the rich historical and architectural heritage, the modern city's social life has roots in the past. To an outsider, these ties seem remarkably close but if they are, it is understandable—a number of benevolent and welfare societies founded before 1750 are still active.

Among them is the St. Andrew's Society, which was organized in 1729 by residents of Scot descent "to assist all people in distress." Before the Revolution, civic-conscious residents had founded the Charleston Library Society, the Charleston Museum (the nation's oldest city museum), and the St. Cecelia Society. The latter, begun as a music group in 1762, first devoted itself to dancing in 1822 when there was a shortage of musicians. The St. Cecilia Ball is now held each year in January, a brilliant social occasion on the local calendar.

In the section of the country long noted for its hospitality, it may well be that Charleston made that reputation for the South. Entertaining guests, and being entertained, is an enjoyment long practiced by residents. For many years, Race Week was Charleston's most important and festive event. Shops closed and business came to a standstill when the fine blooded horses were brought to race for fame—and sometimes for small fortunes.

Diaries and letters from all but the most tragic times recount dinners, balls, parties of all descriptions—with the elegant and distinctive cuisine always an important part of the festivities. Fine cellars were kept by all who could afford them. Madeira was the favorite wine, and, from all accounts, it was consumed in quantity with other spirits; one visitor exclaimed that nowhere else had he been served such rich wines.

Along with the wine and spirits, there is a cuisine that is particularly Charleston in both ingredients and preparation. (For those who would try their talents in preparing Charleston dishes, *Charleston Receipts* is an admirable source of instruction.) Epicures admire many of the dishes, but have extra plaudits for "She-Crab Soup".

The essence of Charleston's charm is not in architecture and customs alone. A touring Rhode Islander, Elkanah Watson, noted after the Revolution that the place had an "almost Asiatic splendor." One modern scholar has called it "the sensuous city", whose natural beauties have endured through the generations—a place with sights, sounds, tastes, and aromas all its own. It is washed by the smells of rivers and marshes and sea mists. It is noteworthy, perhaps, that even the smallest gardens usually have aromatic flowering shrubs.

Solid window shutters keep out harsh sunlight and provide privacy to houses that abut the sidewalks. These were photographed on Church Street.

21 Cumberland Street. Old Powder Magazine. The only public building known to have survived from the days of the Lords Proprietors, this sturdy structure stood inside the walls that originally encompassed the city. Designed to store powder, the walls are two feet eight inches thick and are capped by a groined vaulting of brick and oyster shell mortar.

The basic construction is of "tabby", an early building material made by burning oyster shells to obtain lime, then mixed with shells to form an excellent and durable concrete.

The magazine is owned and operated as a museum by the National Society of the Colonial Dames of America in The State of South Carolina.

There is an almost endless breath of fragrance from gardens—winter-sweet and jasmine, daphne and banana shrub, tea olive and pittosporum, sweet bay and magnolia, loquat and wisteria, jessamine and honeysuckle.

The blend of enticing sounds was little changed before the age of the automobile—endless calls of shore and song birds, ships in harbor, lapping water, pounding surf, the musical accents of Negro voices (in early days contrasting with a Babel of English, French, Portuguese, Dutch, Spanish and the burrs of Scots merchants and gutturals of Cherokee Chiefs).

To be sure, it was never all beauty and sweet scents. A seaport, busy and

Graceful wrought iron affords a sense of privacy, but does not block the view of passersby into this garden on lower Church Street.

prosperous, has, by its very nature, a bitter side. Charleston has had her share; a devoted community is trying, and with success, to clear away the scars of neglect and preserve its abundant beauty.

Many a visitor to Charleston carries away a vision of mellowing houses and narrow streets set amid a vast garden of tropical luxuriance, walled, fenced and hedged, but barely contained.

The gardening tradition is almost as old as the first settlement.

In 1682, two years after the city was moved to the present site, one Thomas Ash recorded that: "Gardens begin to be supplied with such European plants and Herbs as are necessary for the Kitchen . . . Gardens also begin to be beautiful and adorned with such Herbs and Flowers which to the Smell or Eye are pleasing and agreeable, viz. the Rose, Tulip, Carnation and Lilly, etc."

No American city has a richer horticultural tradition. Numerous talented botanists and landscape architects of the 17th and 18th centuries came here to work, drawn by the rich variety of the native flora.

The first gardeners transplanted trees and shrubs of the countryside—live oaks, magnolias, bays, palmettoes, wild fruits, hollies, dogwood, redbud, shadbush, silverbell, deciduous azaleas, yuccas, witch hazel, fringe trees, sweet pepperbush, button bush, red buckeye. Luxuriant vines from the woodlands soon scrambled over garden walls—yellow jessamine, coral honeysuckle, trumpet creeper, crossvine, and the pale blue clematis known locally as "Travelling Joy".

By 1710 the English historian John Lawson was describing these wonders to his countrymen back home, and he was followed by Mark Catesby, "the Colonial Audubon", a self-trained artist sent out by Sir Hans Sloane, founder of the British Museum.

Catesby introduced to England many Carolina exotics, including the magnolia, whose foot-wide blooms opened on a Devonshire estate as early as 1735, to the delight of its owner, Sir John Colleton: "Its ample and fragrant blossoms, the curious structure of its purple cones and pendant scarlet seeds, successively adorn and perfume the woods from May to October." From Charleston, Catesby did much of the exploration that resulted in his masterpiece, *The Natural History of Carolina, Florida and the Bahama Islands.*

There were also the father-and-son botanists from Philadelphia, John and William Bartram. John corresponded and exchanged plants and seeds with Charleston gardeners, and William set out from the city on his exploration of the Deep South in 1773 of which he wrote his celebrated *Travels Through North and South Carolina.*

Most famous of Charleston's early botanists was André Michaux, who arrived in 1786 to collect specimens for the French government. He bought a tract of some 100 acres outside the city as a nursery, and shipped home more than 6000 plants—few of which survived. He also imported plants that were to become so familiar that the South adopted them as its own: crepe myrtle, mimosa, chinaberry and the fragrant tea olive. By tradition it was also Michaux who introduced *Camellia japonica* and the Indian azaleas, which have become the chief ingredients of beauty in the Low Country garden landscapes.

An amateur Charleston botanist, Dr. Alexander Garden, who introduced many native plants to cultivation, became so expert that his correspondent, the great Swedish taxonomist Linnaeus, named the fragrant Chinese native, the *Gardenia,* in his honor.

Many others helped to form the city's gardening traditions: Dr. Thomas Dale, who arrived in 1725; Dr. Thomas Walter, who planted one of the first American botanical gardens outside the city and wrote the most complete 18th century work of its kind, *Flora Caroliniana . . .,* a book that described about 1000 species (Governor John Drayton, himself an amateur botanist, translated Walter's work from the Latin); Joel R. Poinsett, who introduced from Mexico the vividly-colored plant known as *Poinsettia.*

Charleston's private gardens developed rapidly through these generations of horticultural activity. By 1734 a landscape architect from London, Peter Chassereau, was laying out "grounds for Gardens or Parks in a grand and rural manner" and a successor soon offered his services for building fountains, waterworks, grottoes and vineyards. Even earlier, in 1732, "the best garden seeds" had been offered for sale in *The South Carolina Gazette.* Importers also sold a variety of bulbs and

31 Meeting Street. Several water fountains, similar to this one, add to a feeling of repose.

roots: tulips, anemones, narcissus, tuberoses, hyacinths, poppies, carnations and roses.

Local nurserymen served several gardeners of the city and nearby plantations. In 1745 Richard Lake's Ashley River nursery offered "Lemon Trees with Lemons on them in Boxes, Lime Trees and Orange Trees." Twenty years later activity had become so brisk that John Watson, a British gardener for Henry Laurens, sold not only seeds, plants and roots, but also "spades, rakes, reels, lines, watering pots, scythes, furniture and rub-stones, garden and Dutch hoes, watering engines, budding and pruning knives."

The merchant Laurens and his wife, enthusiastic gardeners, imported plants from many parts of the world: olives, capers, limes, ginger, the Alpine strawberry, raspberries, blue grapes, fine French apples, plums and pears.

The earliest Charleston examples have gone the way of most ancient gardens, but though plantings and walkways and even walls disappeared without leaving traces, many accurate garden drawings have been preserved. Many are to be seen in the Charleston Museum and several have been published. Largely due to the skill, devotion, scholarship and unwavering determination of Miss Emma Richardson, many of today's gardens are accurate reflections of their predecessors in design, horticultural material and in spirit.

Though the formal designs of most Charleston gardens reflect their English and European (particularly French) heritage, with their box-bordered paths, geometrically proportioned beds, brick walls and iron gates, the adaptations are Charleston's own. In the luxuriance of their growth through the long, slow seasons, their endless variety of form, color, texture and fragrance, the gardens of the old city are distinctive; a visitor is tempted to say unique.

Charleston's international fame as a garden center was largely won by the incomparable landscapes of great plantation gardens outside the city—in particular, Middleton Place, Magnolia and Cypress Gardens. These three attractions alone have drawn millions of visitors from many parts of the world.

Middleton Place, with its butterfly lakes, great drifts of azaleas and allées of camellias, is the oldest landscaped garden in the country. When the invading Federal troops swept through the area, the plantation house was burned and the Middleton family could no longer maintain the property. After years of neglect, Middleton Place has once more become one of the great gardens of the world.

Magnolia Gardens, situated near Middleton Place, was originally

Live oaks, usually festooned with Spanish moss, thrive in the semi-tropical Charleston climate. This beauty hugs the shore of the Ashley River, on the grounds of Magnolia Gardens.

named for a magnificent row of magnolia trees stretching to the river. Pre-World War I Baedekers for the United States listed three two-star items for travellers: the Grand Canyon, Niagara Falls and Magnolia Gardens.

Cypress Gardens was planted more recently; in the 18th century, the lake was a "reserve" used for flooding the fields by a rice planter. Masses of azaleas and flowering spring bulbs are reflected in the inky, still waters; overhead, the great cypress trees sift the sunlight.

Middleton Place and Magnolia Gardens are on the Ashley River, Cypress Gardens on the Cooper River. To professional and amateur botanists, and to lovers of beauty, all three come close to being shrines.

Preservation of Charleston's historic houses and buildings is successful and continuing. A great deal remains to be done, but it requires time, money and effort. Archaeological studies are in progress on several sites, and planning for future projects is the concern of both individuals and organizations.

This great effort is being made not only for Charleston and her residents, but for all Americans.

87 Church Street. Heyward-Washington House. The three-story brick house in the center of the picture was built by a wealthy rice planter, Daniel Heyward. The interior, finished in fine cypress paneling, houses a notable collection of Charleston furniture.

George Washington was a guest here on his official Southern tour in 1791.

Before restoration, this historic house had been defaced by a baker who installed a plate glass window; the kitchen had been used as a pool hall. Now owned by the Charleston Museum, the main house, kitchen and garden are open to the public. Admission fee.

On the right (89-91 Church Street) is Catfish Row, of Dubose Heyward's *Porgy*.

"... the most
civilized town
in the world."

38-40-44 Tradd Street. (right to left)
Almost all the dwellings in this block
date to colonial times; they barely
escaped the disastrous fire of 1778 that
destroyed many of the pre-
Revolutionary buildings. Two of the
earliest in this group date to 1718. The
street may have been named for the first
male child born in the young city.

Gardens in the rear of the Heyward-Washington House are laid out in typical eighteenth century style. Perhaps because of their memories of English gardens, colonists liked and used the formal, stylized use of boxwood. This garden was designed by Miss Emma Richardson. It is maintained by the Garden Club of Charleston.

One of the finest pieces of furniture ever made in America, the secretary-bookcase in the Heyward-Washington House combines Chippendale and Hepplewhite styles. It was made locally, although the cabinetmaker responsible is not known. The books on its shelves were gathered from local private libraries; many of them bear the 18th century bookplates of John Bee Holmes, an early owner of the bookcase. This piece is known as the "Holmes breakfront".

The mahogany breakfast table, and also the chairs, date from 1760 to 1790 and are attributed to Thomas Elfe.

Thomas Elfe, one of the most prolific and talented Charleston cabinetmakers, produced fretwork like this over a mantel of the Heyward-Washington House. Several other similar pieces are attributed to Elfe.

51 Meeting Street. Nathaniel Russell House. The prosperous merchant, who came from
Rhode Island to Charleston before the Revolution, had completed this house by 1809.
The main structure is of Carolina gray brick trimmed with red brick. Russell's initials can

be seen in the cartouche of the front panel of the wrought iron balcony which is continuous and extends across the front and side of the house.

This imposing home, built at the enormous cost of $80,000, boasts oval, square and rectangular rooms, and Adam style mantels, overdoors and overwindows. The furnishings are of the period.

Historic Charleston Foundation acquired the house in 1955 and has its headquarters here. Open to the public year around with an admission fee.

A dramatic view of the free-flying spiral stairway of the Nathaniel Russell House, one of the architectural gems of the city. This striking photograph was taken from the third floor.

Steeple, St. Michael's Church. The clock and eight bells in this steeple were installed in 1764. The clock is the "official" timepiece for the city. Although the church building survived the 1886 earthquake, the 186-foot-high steeple sank eight inches from the tremor.

80 Broad Street. City Hall, seen through a window of St. Michael's Church. Designed by Gabriel Manigault, Charleston's "gentleman architect", in 1801, this building was acquired by the city in 1818. Of special interest are the bull's eye grills and the two rear basement window grills, of wrought iron.

St. Michael's is the oldest church building in the city, although not the oldest parish. Its cornerstone was laid in 1752 and the first services were held in 1761. Samuel Cardy is thought to have been the architect.

The "defects" in the two St. Michael's window panes are marks left by the glassblower's pipe.

21 East Battery. Edmondston-Alston House. Now open to the public as a house museum of Historic Charleston Foundation, this elegant town house was built about 1828 by Charles Edmondston. Charles Alston, a Georgetown County rice planter, purchased the house ten years later.

The house, with elaborate and unconventional woodwork, also contains a fine collection of Alston family furnishings.

Books in the Edmondston-Alston library have not left the residence since they were acquired; most of them are now collectors' items. The furniture here, like that in the rest of the house, is part of the Alston family collection.

83-108 East Bay. Rainbow Row. An arched passage frames a magnificent wrought iron gate in this colorful row of buildings. When eighteenth century merchants built here, gateways led to gardens, from which private stairways rose to the second

story living quarters. There was no access from the first floor shop directly to the second floor.

The buildings are derivative of both English and Dutch architecture and were erected between 1720 and 1787. In Colonial times, they fronted directly on the water, giving the merchants quick and easy access to nearby ships.

99-101 East Bay. This is an interior of the first of the row houses to be restored on what is now known as "Rainbow Row". The restoration took place in 1932 after the entire block had deteriorated into slums.

The private dwelling contains a number of Charleston-made pieces, some of them shown here. The library walls, paneled in cypress, were stripped of many coats of paint during the restoration.

The Sword Gates, at 32 Legare Street. This famous iron work was done by Christopher Werner in the nineteenth century, who originally designed the gates for the city.

94 Rutledge Avenue. Mikell House. A prosperous Edisto Island cotton planter, Isaac Jenkins Mikell, built this 1853 house as a wedding present for his third bride. Used as a winter residence until the War Between the States, the building is one of the finest examples of Greek Revival architecture in the city. The extensive gardens have been restored to the period of the house.

Ram's head capitals atop the six composite columns of the Mikell House.

27 King Street. Miles Brewton House. Completed in 1769, this has been called "perhaps the finest Colonial town house in America". Certainly, it is one of the finest Georgian houses ever erected in this country. Miles Brewton was both wealthy and influential; he was a member of the Commons House of Assembly for many years.

The British commander, Gen. Sir Henry Clinton, lived here when the city was occupied during the Revolution, and the Union Generals Hatch and Meade made it headquarters during the War Between the States.

The house and courtyard dependencies, remaining unaltered, present an accurate 18th century picture.

Admired in the 18th century as one of the truly beautiful and perfect rooms in the country, the Miles Brewton drawing room has lost none of its charm through the centuries. The Irish crystal chandelier, still lit by candles, dominates the large room that stretches almost the entire width of the second floor front of the mansion.

Detail of the carved woodwork which is found throughout the Miles Brewton house. Such magnificent work helps explain why the house took ten years to build.

A rear view of the Miles Brewton house, showing (on the left) the 18th century servants' quarters and kitchens, and a corner of the formal garden. The garden, whose striking box-bordered beds are of 18th century design, is part of the larger original which once extended to the water.

64 South Battery. William Gibbes House. The marble stairway on the front facade was added to this 1772 house in 1800. Considered of national importance, this large home is a fine example of Georgian architecture. The second floor drawing room is regarded as one of the most beautiful rooms in the country.

17 Chalmers Street. The Pink House. This appealing small building, one of the most-photographed of Charleston originals, is believed to have been a tavern in the Colonial period. The tile roof is characteristic of early Charleston.

The East Battery at high tide. For almost three centuries Charlestonians labored to reclaim the marshy waterfront along the Cooper River, filling with stones and other heavy material after each major storm. Finally, this masonry barrier was completed, holding back the raging waters that gale winds often fling at the city's vulnerable perimeter.

7-9 Stoll's Alley. Justinius Stoll built No. 7 (in the foreground) in the mid-18th century and this charming narrow passageway bears his name. The adjoining house is also pre-Revolutionary.

Corner, East Battery and South Battery. An Oleander (Nerium oleander) in full bloom. The plant was first introduced into England from Southern Europe in 1596, and brought to Charleston by the city's early gardeners, perhaps before the end of the seventeenth century. Very much at home in Charleston's climate, the oleander blooms throughout most of the summer.

106 Broad Street. Lining House. Dr. John Lining's house narrowly escaped the great fire of 1861. The oldest wooden building in the city, it was used as an apothecary shop from 1780 until 1962, when it was restored by the Preservation Society of Charleston.

Dr. Lining made the first scientific weather observations in the country.

110 Broad Street. Harvey House. Constructed prior to 1728 by William Harvey, this twelve-room house has been called an "architectural museum piece." It has remained virtually unchanged, and in the same family, since it was built.

Much of the floor-to-ceiling paneling is very wide; there are three-foot-wide planks over several mantels. There are also many unusual building features: six-foot-wide hinged doors, chimneys that provide their usual function but also act as beam supports, door frames set into arched openings.

172 Rutledge Avenue. Ashley Hall. Built as a residence by Patrick Duncan about 1815 and occupied for several years by George A. Trenholm, treasurer of the Confederate States, Ashley Hall has been in use as a private girls' school since 1909.

The interior is distinguished by a spiral staircase soaring from the ground floor to the roof, and by magnificent carved woodwork and paneling. The ground floor piazza, originally open, was enclosed in comparatively recent years.

631 East Bay Street. Faber House. This 1839 Palladian mansion, suffering from damage and neglect that began during the city's occupation by Union forces in 1865, was saved by the Historic Charleston Foundation. Now restored, it houses business offices. The hexagonal cupola still provides a vantage spot to view the harbor; in early days, tidal creeks flowed by the portico.

42 Society Street. The perfectly scaled furnishings of this dining room include an English tazza and claret jugs of about 1800 on an octagonal English table dating from the first half of the 18th century. The barometer, also English, was made by Robert Masefield in 1767. The portrait is an early 19th century likeness of Arthur Middleton of Stono.

64 Meeting Street. A small town garden at the peak of azalea season, with hyacinths and tulips also in bloom. The handsome tree on the left is a crepe myrtle, often unfamiliar to visitors to the South. The residence is a typical single house with a secluded piazza.

21 King Street. Patrick O'Donnell House. This typically Charleston tier of soaring piazzas is attached to an Italian Renaissance style residence. Built by an Irish master mason, the main house was completed about 1856. Of special note are the facade's decorative details. Unusually well constructed, the central portion survived the 1886 earthquake. The older library wing suffered such damage that it had to be rebuilt in 1887.

The Exchange Building. Although it has not been as well publicized as the Boston Tea Party, Charles Town had its protest against the tax on tea which had been levied by the British Parliament. The protest meeting was held in the Great Hall of the Exchange Building on Dec. 3, 1773, following the arrival in port of a consignment of 257 chests of tea on board the *London.* At the meeting, three consignees of the cargo were asked to agree not to accept the shipment; they agreed. Later, a second meeting was held and a resolution passed that no tea would be "landed, received or vended" until the taxation on tea was repealed.

Charleston's most historic building was then sparkling new. Begun in 1767, it had been completed in 1771 by Peter and John Horlbeck on plans drawn by Thomas Woodin.

St. Philip's Steeple, from the western churchyard. The first wrought iron gates to the yard had strong reminders of man's frailty—including skull and crossbones, which were replaced by more conventional decorations that date from the 18th century.

St. Philip's steeple and St. Michael's steeple dominate the skyline of the old city.

Viewed from this vantage point, the unusual use of three porticos on the church edifice is apparent.

146 Church Street. St. Philip's Church. Although this is the oldest Protestant Episcopal congregation in South Carolina, the building dates from 1838. The first St. Philip's was a small wooden structure on the site of the present St. Michael's.

William Rhett, nemesis of the pirates, presented the congregation with communion silver that is still in use. The building was badly damaged during the War Between the States.

Church Street traffic bends around the St. Philip's portico that juts beyond the sidewalk.

350 Meeting Street. Joseph Manigault House. Gabriel Manigault designed this Adam style house for his brother about 1803. One of the best examples of his work, it was offered for sale for non-payment of taxes in 1933. It was purchased by Princess Pignatelli as an early preservation effort and given to the Charleston Museum.

The form is that of a parallelogram, with bows on the north and east sides, and a bowed piazza on the west. A lovely circular stair, fitted into the north bow, rises from a wide central hallway.

The house has been furnished in impeccable fashion. Open to the public.

The drawing room of the Joseph Manigault house is furnished, like other rooms in the mansion, with period furniture. The set of chairs and sofa, with painted scenes, reputedly was used by Thomas Pinckney when he served at the Court of St. James from 1792 to 1796.

The portrait is of Elizabeth Wragg Manigault, painted in 1757 by Charleston's "court painter" Jeremiah Theus.

An upper story view of the gate house entrance to the grounds of Joseph Manigault house. The garden site was occupied by a service station before it was rescued and restored on the original plan; luckily, a drawing of the garden had been made before it was destroyed.

The only other gate house in the city is the massive one at the College of Charleston.

Rice grown in the low country brought wealth to planters and to Charleston, and it was honored in decorative pieces. Here, a bedpost of a valuable "rice bed" in the Joseph Manigault house.

116 Broad Street. Rutledge House. A 19th century architect made many changes in the facade of this house which dates prior to the Revolution. The magnificent wrought iron by Christopher Werner, one of the most gifted of all Charleston ironworkers, was added, as were the window cornices. This was the home of John Rutledge, for a time "president" of the independent republic of South Carolina, governor of the state, a state chief justice and congressman.

39 Church Street. Eveleigh House. George Eveleigh, a fur trader, built this Georgian house in 1743. Though it was damaged by a hurricane nine years later and lost its roof in an 1811 tornado, little damage was suffered by the interior, which remains almost unchanged.

135 Church Street. Dock Street Theatre. The home of the Footlight Players of Charleston, this attractive building is on the same land occupied by a theatre that was erected in 1736. Later, it was the site of the famous Planter's Hotel which fell into ruins following the War Between the States. The present reconstructed building is owned by the city and was opened in 1937 with a production by the community theatre group.

A great deal of the material from the Planter's Hotel is incorporated in the reconstruction.

14 Legare Street. "Pineapple Gates". The finials are actually pine cones carved by nineteenth-century Italian stonemasons—in response to the owner's request for live oak acorns!

70 Tradd Street. There are many family heirlooms in this dining room of a private residence. The corner cupboard holds china which once belonged to Arthur Middleton. The portrait is of Humphrey Courtney, shown holding the bill of lading for perhaps the first cotton shipped from Charles Town.

54 Queen Street. Thomas Elfe House. This miniature single house once was owned by Charleston's most renowned cabinetmaker, Thomas Elfe. Because of the many fine details, it is believed he may have built the house.

The house has remarkably fine proportions and is unique among 18th century buildings. The chair rail is three inches lower than normal—making the ceilings appear higher. The cypress woodwork is comparable to fine furniture.

58 Church Street. The glory of azaleas surrounding a small reflecting pool and a planting of newly-green boxwood.

59 Church Street. A privately owned house, built about 1735, is a showplace of eighteenth century pieces of varied background. The magnificent needlepoint is original. On the left wall is an eighteenth-century Adam style commode in satinwood.

59 Meeting Street. Branford-Horry House and garden in spring.
Passersby can see this lovely informal garden through the porthole-like
opening in the gate. The house is pre-Revolutionary, the portico a later
addition.

54 Hasell Street. William Rhett House. The oldest house extant in Charleston, this home was completed about 1712 by the doughty colonel who led a party to capture the pirate Stede Bonnet and his men. The entrance stairs and piazzas are later additions.

This house narrowly escaped two major fires that took many pre-Revolutionary buildings.

When Charleston was a walled city, an avenue of trees led to the North Gate from this plantation house.

18 Bull Street. Blacklock House. Distinguished workmanship abounds in this
fine double house of Carolina brick. The English red rubbed brick used in the
arches are fitted with such skill that the joints are almost paper thin.

William Blacklock, one of the many residents who acquired wealth during
an era of commercial expansion, completed this residence in 1800. Among his
prominent contemporaries were Nathaniel Russell and Joseph Manigault.

53 Meeting Street. First (Scots) Presbyterian Church, with its prominent steeples, is shown in this view taken from St. Michael's steeple. The church was organized in 1731 by twelve Scottish families; the first building was erected in 1734. This building is the fifth oldest church edifice in the city. It was damaged by the hurricane of 1885, the earthquake of 1886, a tornado in 1938 and a fire in 1945. The burning bush (copied from the Seal of the Church of Scotland) is in the window over the main doorway.

Flower Vendors. In earlier days, hucksters musically chanted their merchandise as they led horse-drawn wagons through the streets, a custom that survives only in the selling of flowers on street corners.

8 Archdale Street. Unitarian Church. Home of the oldest Unitarian congregation in the South, this building was near completion at the outbreak of the Revolution. Part of the Independent Church of Charleston, it broke away from that church in 1817 and became a Unitarian Church in 1837.

   Extensively remodeled and enlarged in 1852-54, the interior is modeled after the Henry VII Chapel in Westminster Abbey.

188 Meeting Street. Market Hall. Though somewhat overwhelming when viewed close-up, the stately proportions of this building become obvious and impressive from a distance. Designed by E. B. White, it is now the headquarters of the Charleston Chapter of the Daughters of the Confederacy. A second-floor museum is open to the public.

The ground floor contains shops. This is one of the few remaining 19th century market complexes in the country.

66 George Street. College of Charleston. The first municipal college in the country, this institution was chartered in 1786. The main building, designed by William Strickland, dates from 1828, but the portico and wings were added in 1850 by E. B. White, who also designed the porter's lodge.

136 Church Street. Huguenot Church. E. B. White designed this neo-Gothic edifice that dates from 1844, the third Huguenot Church to occupy the same site. The first was built about 1681. In Colonial times, services were scheduled so that planters could travel in large canoes to and from their Cooper River plantations with the tides.

6 Chalmers Street. Old Slave
Mart. The small central building,
which was built by Thomas Ryan
and his partner about 1853, was
used for public and private
auctions of lands, carriages, horses,
furniture and ships' cargoes—
including slaves. The building was
opened as a museum in 1938; an
exhibit of crafts that were taught to
slaves is on display.

Even such primitive paving as
cobblestones, now relaid in
cement, was not known until after
the Revolution. Ladies wore clogs
to escape the mud and even
horses had a sort of clog on their
hooves.

34 Meeting Street. Huger House and Garden. A shade-dappled lawn lends a sense of spaciousness and serenity to this garden in azalea season. The house, built in 1760, was occupied by Lord William Campbell, the last of the Royal Governors of South Carolina.

42 State Street. A towering Magnolia grandiflora against a brick wall (left background) dominates this informal garden that also features a small reflecting pool. Another tree that thrives in the Southern sun is the crepe myrtle (right foreground). Camellias in full bloom are proof that the picture was taken in early spring; Charleston's semi-tropical climate allows winter only a short stay. The urns were at one time on the Exchange Building.

100 Tradd Street. This view of the cloistered garden is framed by a live oak and plantings of native bamboo. Early roses are coming into bloom. Designed by Loutrel W. Briggs, whose book, *Charleston Gardens*, is a definitive study of the city's gardens and horticultural history.

West Point Rice Mill, shown from across the Municipal Yacht Basin. Now used for offices, this is one of two rice mills left standing. In the years when rice culture was at it height, this was one of the busiest places in Charleston.

Charlestowne Landing. A facsimile of a trading ketch used in the period when settlers were being brought, under the Lords Proprietors, to establish a city in the New World. The first settlement began in 1670 when three small ships arrived here on the banks of the Ashley River.

Now an historic park site, Charlestowne Landing is open to the public on a fee basis.

Route 61. Drayton Hall. This magnificent Palladian house is under the aegis of the National Trust for Historic Preservation. Since none of the original construction has been disturbed by installation of 19th or 20th century improvements, the former Low Country plantation house is a treasure not only for its beauty but its authenticity.

Every room in the house is paneled from floor to ceiling. The single most striking exterior feature is the portico with Doric and Ionic columns of Portland stone that was imported from England.

Route 61. Magnolia Gardens. One of the show place gardens of the world; there are over 1,000 varieties of camellias planted on these extensive grounds. Originally called Magnolia on the Ashley, because of the long line of magnolia trees that led from the river to the house, the land was first owned and developed by the Drayton family.

Open to the public, on a fee basis, in the spring.

Route 61. Middleton Place. It was here that Andre Michaux introduced the first camellias to the United States in the 18th century; several of his original plantings remain. The oldest landscaped garden in this country, it was part of the rice plantation of the Middleton family.

Following the Civil War, when the house was burned, the gardens were neglected. But one hundred and ten acres are on the Register of National Historic Landmarks and have been rescued from overgrowth and returned to their former grandeur. The gardens, house and stableyards are open to the public for a fee, year round.

—*Photo courtesy Middleton Place.*

Route 52. Cypress Gardens, once a fresh-water reserve for a rice plantation. Visitors to these gardens may be taken in boats over the cypress-darkened waters. There also are meandering paths, bordered by heavy plantings of azaleas.

Now owned by the city of Charleston, the gardens are open in the spring for a fee.

–Photo courtesy South Carolina Department of Parks, Recreation and Tourism

A late afternoon stroll along the Battery—a traditional rite among Charlestonians.

Design by Richard Stinely